FROM A DOUBTER TO A DREAMER

Overcome Your Fears and Live Your DREAMS!

KISHMA A. GEORGE

FOREWORD BY: LES BROWN

From a Doubter to a Dreamer Copyright © August 2020
By Kishma A. George

Published in the United States of America by
ChosenButterflyPublishing LLC

www.cb-publishing.com
Editing by Stephanie Montgomery, Unique Communications Concepts
Cover design CTS Graphic Designs

All rights reserved under International Copyright Law. Contents and/or cover may not be reproduced, distributed, or transmitted in any form or by any means or stored in a database or retrieval system, without the prior written consent of the publisher and/or authors.

ISBN: 978-1-945377-15-0
Hard Copy Edition
Printed in the United States of America
August 2020

Books also Featuring Kishma A. George

When New Life Begins

Bringing Forth the Dreamer in You

Dreaming the Dream

The Princess in You

Table of Contents

- Foreword by Les Brown .... Pg 7
- Chapter One: A Divine Touch .... Pg 11
- Chapter Two: Yielding to God's Plan ... Pg 21
- Chapter Three: The Process .... Pg 27
- Chapter Four: Faith at Work .... Pg 31
- Chapter Five: Dream Again .... Pg 35
- Chapter Six: Just Believe .... Pg 39
- Chapter Seven: Hold Fast to the Vision .. Pg 43
- Chapter Eight: God Is All You Need .... Pg 47
- Chapter Nine: A VISION Becomes Reality Pg 53
- Prophetic Release .... Pg 61
- Prophetic Prayer for Dreamers .... Pg 69
- Living Your Dreams Journal .... Pg 71
- About the Author .... Pg 91
- Acknowledgements .... Pg 95
- About K.I.S.H. Home, Inc. .... Pg 99

Foreword by Les Brown

Have you ever had a dream and you talked YOU out of it? After you get excited and have a plan of action, you then begin to give yourself every reason why it won't work. Here's what I've learned, for every dream, there's automatically resistance. Automatically! Don't let the resister be you...The truth of the matter is, you are well equipped to handle the fiery furnaces of life. The truth of the matter is, you are more than a conqueror. The truth of the matter is, greater is He that is in me...I know I am never, ever alone!

From a Doubter to a Dreamer is one of my favorites, because Kishma had every reason to doubt herself, her vision, and to retreat to life's woes. Instead, she persisted. Instead, she bent but refuse to break. Instead, she allowed God to use her to heal and deliver many others who are stuck and now free because Kishma became a dreamer and doer of her calling.

I dare you to find the courage to dream and I double dare you to find the strength to execute the dream and vision placed in your spirit. You hear it and you try to ignore it. Just like I did. It took me more than 20 years to have the courage and step out on faith to speak to millions to let them know, You have greatness in you, You've gotta be hungry, and to Live full, and Die empty.

From a Doubter to a Dreamer will give you the encouragement you need to fulfill the calling on your life.

I'm speaking from the most humble experience...It's Possible!

Les Brown

www.lesbrown.com

Chapter One:
A Divine Touch

Can you imagine me, your girl Kishma - a doubter? I know many of you are saying, "Kishma, a doubter?" I know many are wondering, "How could that be possible?" For all the things I have accomplished so far in life, many of you probably find it very hard to believe that I was a doubter. Yes, it is true, I was once a BIG doubter; living in fear, having low self-esteem, having my mind set on my own dreams - not on God-given dreams and very confused about my destiny. However, God brought me from being a BIG doubter to now being a BIG dreamer. Let me share my story with you.

Several years ago, I had my life all planned out after graduating from Charlotte Amalie High School in St. Thomas, United States Virgin Islands. My dreams were to be married at the age of 25 - receive my Master's degree, have five children and shop until I drop. I was so excited about living my dreams.

I began dating a man who was thirteen years older than I was. He was very charming and handsome and he caught my eye because his presence was breath taking. I met him at my first job, after I graduated from high school. He paid all my bills and bought me whatever I wanted. In my mind I thought I had arrived, it was like a dream come true!

I did not grow up poor, but I felt a need for more money because I was able to get what I really wanted to buy without being on a budget and I also wanted to fit in with my friends who dated older men.

I was brought up simply in a home with both parents and a younger brother. Mom was a no-nonsense woman, whereas Dad (now deceased) in my opinion was the coolest and most reasonable man on the earth. I rather dealt with my Dad because he was more cooperative. I just loved going to him for permission for things that had absolutely nothing to do with school. Anything and everything with my education was Mom's territory.

Mom made me feel that I had to be perfect in everything. I hated that! No matter the time or place she was always in the mood to reprimand me and put me in my place. Numerous times she got off the main road and parked in order to deal with me. It was like I could never get anything done correctly. I must confess that she was always ready to give me a helping hand. In fact, she gave too much help. She had a tutor for just about every subject during the school year and summer were so boring with summer school to prepare for the coming school year. I wanted a break. I hated books!! Oh, how I hated anything that required studying.

I wanted a change and I got it when I least expected it. One day Mom set me loose and expected me to do more on my own. I did not know why the change came about until she shared with me what my 12th grade science teacher told her. Mom told him that I was very lazy. However, he disagreed big time with her. He said that I was not by any means lazy but that I would not do anything for myself that I can get someone else to do for me. She said that after hearing that she applied the advice. She said that she could not have gotten a better advice from a teacher.

When I announced to her in my senior year that I wanted to attend college off island, she paid me no mind. I needed help. Lots of help with applications. Well, she gave none! You would have thought that she would help me. She did not so much as pick up her little finger to assist me. She declared that if I really wanted to go to college on the mainland, I would get it done by helping myself.

I really, really wanted to leave my parents' home. So, I worked very hard for about a year and a half and saved money for my ticket. My money! I purchased my own ticket with no help. Mom did me a favor by doing the easiest thing, she picked up my ticket from the travel agency. Leave it to Mom, I would have traveled to the USA solo. However, Dad insisted that Mom should accompany me. She listened and accompanied me to Dover, Delaware to register at Delaware State University.

At the university, I made a few friends that I held on too tightly and feared to let go. I had such a low opinion of myself that I thought their ideas were always far better than mine. They were the leaders and I being the follower. They always led, and I simply followed. I did little or no thinking on my own. They had me just where they wanted. If they said jump I would ask like a fool, "How high." I thought that they were my friends and would not do anything that was not for my best interest. This friendship was broken at God's chosen time. Later on, I no longer associated with them because they were not helping me to bloom. Rather I was stagnant in my growth and self-esteem was low. They were glooming with self-esteem but not me.

Meanwhile, I continued my relationship after several months of dating with this guy even after I moved to Delaware to attend my first year in college. I had concerns with our relationship being long distance. He told me not to worry about anything because he loved me and wanted to marry me. As the months went by, my friends from the Virgin Islands called to tell me they saw my boyfriend hanging out with a woman. When I heard the news, I brushed it off because I thought my friends were just jealous.

Then I started to receive more phone calls about my boyfriend hanging around this woman. One day I got so frustrated, I called and confronted him about the rumors I was hearing. During the conversation, there was a long silence. He paused, said he had something to tell me - but it could not be discussed over the phone. He said that he really loved me and did not want to lose me and that he would take a trip to Delaware to talk about what was really going on. Days went by while I waited to see my boyfriend and I was still getting phone calls about him hanging out with this woman! In my mind, I was saying it was not true and that he loves me - but deep down inside I felt like something was not right!

The month approached for my boyfriend to visit me in Delaware. We went out to dinner that night when he arrived. During dinner, we talked about everything under the sun; nothing pertaining to the rumors I heard about him. As we arrived back to the apartment, he sat me down and broke down that he was seeing another woman, but he did not love her. He then wrapped his arms around my shoulder to comfort me before he said his final word.

He looked into my eyes, said he was very sorry for the pain and hurt he caused me - but there was something else he had to share. As he continued to talk, he got closer and closer while rubbing my shoulders and hugging me. Then he whispered, "I'm still married!" What? I knew I heard wrong! I sobbed loudly. I was so shocked, I asked him to repeat what he said. I pushed him away from me and fell to my knees crying aloud! That was not all; he also said softly that he was expecting a baby in a few months with another woman.

That was all I needed to hear and lay on the floor crying for a few hours. As I laid on the floor, I cried out, "WHY DID YOU LIE TO ME? WHY DIDN'T YOU TELL ME THE TRUTH?" I felt like my whole life and dreams had collapsed. I felt so hurt, angry, disappointed and frustrated. I did not want to live anymore. I wanted to know, how did a girl like me get caught up is such a big mess?? I said to myself, "I was raised in a Christian home with my father, mother and brother. We attended church every Sunday morning and evenings, on Wednesday night for Bible Study and Friday night I attended Young People's Meetings. My parents were very loving and supportive in my childhood life, how in the world did this happen?" The next week he left, and I did not speak to him for several months.

One day while attending class, I began vomiting and feeling very sick and weak. I went to the doctor the same day. Shortly after the doctor entered back into the office, he said my test results were great but there was one thing causing my sickness. I waited with my heart pounding; I could hear my heart - that's how loud it was. The doctor told me I was PREGNANT! OH, NO! The test is wrong! This cannot be happening to me! How can I be pregnant? I started to cry as I left the doctor's office.

I was so afraid to tell my family that I was pregnant because I was raised in church and was taught that before you bring a child into this world, you should be married. I thought my life was over. I went into depression. I sat on my bed every day and cried my heart out. I remember hurting so much inside, that I would tell everyone I met at the store or any place, what I was going through. My heart was so heavy; if a dog walked by, I would start telling the dog about the problems I was dealing with.

Months passed, and I began to get very lonely. I talked to my boyfriend on the phone every day, even though I was not happy with his life style. I continued to stay in the relationship because I was having his child. One day while I was cooking, my doorbell rang. When I opened the door - it was my boyfriend, who had flown all the way from the Virgin Islands to surprise me!

He brought me a dozen of red roses, clothes, jewelry and then handed me a little box with my name on it. When I opened the box, to my surprise, it was a diamond ring - and he asked me to marry him! I asked him if he were still married and he said, "No..." Therefore, my response was "yes" - but deep down inside, I knew it was not a good idea. I began to reason with myself that I always dreamed of marrying, settling down and starting a family; besides, I was carrying his child.

During my pregnancy, I still received phone calls from friends in the Virgins Islands telling me that my boyfriend was hanging with other women. Every time I heard the gossip, I would have labor pains and go straight to the hospital. I visited the hospital so many times that one day a nurse came into my hospital room and asked me what was going on in my life that was stressing me. I explained to her everything that was going on with my child's father.

She looked me directly in my face and said that I needed to get a hold of my life. She told me that I was a beautiful woman and had to know my worth. At this time in my life, my self-esteem was very low. She encouraged me not to pick up the phone when certain friends called with information about my child's father. She also warned me if I delivered my baby too early, my baby would have many health problems. After that day, I never returned to the hospital until it was time to birth my baby.

On January 31, 1997, I gave birth to a beautiful healthy baby girl. One day as I held my daughter in my arms, I made up my mind that I wanted the best for my daughter and me. I felt stuck because my boyfriend - her father, was the provider. He paid all my bills and bought us everything we needed.

With all of the drama going on in my life, I decided to take a vacation and visit my mother in the Virgin Islands. My father had passed away the year before I visited home and my brother moved to California. While visiting my mother I told her I needed help; I was not happy being in the relationship I was in. I felt like he did not know my worth nor loved me the way he should. I knew deep down inside I wanted more, but I thought to myself - how do I come out of this? Who will pay my bills and take care of my child? I didn't think I could take care of myself and my baby because I was not employed. I remember asking my mother how I could really get out. She answered, "Only God can help you." I thought to myself, what kind of mother would give an answer like that?

When my vacation ended, I went back to Delaware. Two weeks later, I received a phone call from a friend and she invited me to attend church with her in Dover, Delaware. When I arrived at the church, I felt as if I belonged there. During the altar call, my friend invited me to go to the altar. When I got to the altar, I heard the Lord speaking to my spirit for the very first time in my life. The Lord said, "Come to me today; I will take care of you!" I began speaking back to the Lord under my breath asking Him, "How can I really come to You today if the guy I'm dating pays all of my bills. Who will take care of me and my child?" The Lord said to me that He would take care of me, to come today! The Lord said, He would never leave me nor forsake me! When I said, "Yes Lord I will come to You today," it felt like a big weight lifted from my shoulders. Before I left the altar, I rededicated my life back to God. It was truly a divine touch from the Lord on that day! It was truly a life-changing experience.

On my way home, the Lord dealt with me. I changed my radio station from secular music to the gospel station. When

I arrived home that day, I received a call from the guy I was dating and I told him I had moved on with my life and that all ties are cut. He asked me who would pay my bills and take care of me. I answered and said, "God will pay and take care of me and my daughter." He laughed and hung up the phone. I felt peace when I hung up.

Several months after I rededicated my life to the Lord, I began reading the Bible and praying. I began to feel comfortable with myself. I began to love myself instead of looking to men to love me! I began to see what God sees! I learned not to wait for people to accept me but realize that God accepts me! I began to find myself. I began to walk, talk, look, act, and think differently! As I continued my walk with God, this transition was hard for me because I had to totally depend on God and not a man.

My journey from dependency, low-self-esteem gradually to blooming to independency, self-confidence and finding my place in the world to make a difference was slowly unwrapping before my eyes. However, I was clueless. Little did I know that the change in being in a larger place would have such an impact in my life. This was the beginning of the NEW ME!!! The beginning of me changing from being so doubtful about myself.

Chapter Two
Yielding to God's Plan

One day as I sat on my bed, I cried out to God. I was so sick and tired of my life situations. I told God there had to be more to life than this. My life was the same routine day by day - living paycheck to paycheck, going to work, church and back home. In that season of my life, I was working at a fast food restaurant although I had a degree in psychology.

Some of my college friends would come in the restaurant and see me mopping the floors and cleaning the toilets. They laughed at me and said it was a shame because I was not motivated to do better. They were so insensitive! Deep down inside, I knew I would not be working in a restaurant for the rest of my life. Why did I feel this way??? What makes me feel this way? That I did not know! So, I kept working at the restaurant until my working hours were reduced to an on-call shift.

One day I went to the grocery store using my food stamps. There I met a young woman who graduated from the same college I attended. She told me about her new job, then asked me the question I dreaded to answer; "Where do you work?" I answered that I was still employed but currently did not have working hours, but I was sending out my résumé and filling out job applications. She then asked what my degree was and I told her psychology. She informed me that there was an agency hiring for a Wraparound Therapist position. She said this job position assisted youth in the foster care system and that I should apply. My reply was that I had no experience working with youth in foster care. She looked at me with a smile and said I could do anything I set my mind to do.

I felt within myself that God was ordering my steps. She gave me the contact information and I faxed my résumé the next day. A few days later, I received a phone call for an interview for the job. I was so excited! I prayed to God the night before that He would give me the right words to say during the interview. The following day, I went to the job interview and was hired on the spot. God was teaching me that when situations look impossible in life - all things are possible with Him and that I should stand still and see the salvation of the Lord!

While working as a Wraparound Therapist, I witnessed the tremendous challenges that youth who aged out of foster care experienced while trying to find their way towards a self-sufficient and stable life. A passion within me grew for the aged-out youth and their future as I experienced their frustration in handling basic skills, such as opening a checking/savings account, parenting and the frustration of being single parents.

Many of the youth I worked with left foster care at the age of 18 years and found themselves homeless, pregnant, lacking self-esteem, incarcerated, unemployed and without guidance. They struggled in their transition of leaving their foster homes because many were still attending high school and were not emotionally or financially stable.

There was one story that really touched my heart. It was then I knew that I wanted to make a difference in the lives of these youth and ensure that they had a safe, successful transition to adulthood and independent living. While working as an Independent Living Mentor, I mentored a young man named Antonio Rasin.

Antonio Rasin was adopted and placed into a foster home during his youth. God was introduced in his life - but due to his gloomy surroundings, Antonio felt as though God did not care about him. God revealed His care through his introduction to me. He states in an article written by Kimberly B. Gladney in K.I.S.H. Magazine, "The things I was going through, I didn't see God nowhere, Kishma was the first person that actually made me feel like God even cared...as far as somebody like me anyway."

He aged out of the foster care system when he turned 18. Turning 18, he had to face the reality of life, but didn't know where to start. He had no home and was now out on the streets of Delaware without a plan. He had just turned 18 years old; I asked the foster mom if he could stay in her home for a while until I could find him a job and a place for him to live. The foster mom said that she would not receive a check for him staying at her home, so he could not stay there because of her income wages.

We left her home that day and I drove around Dover, Delaware until 5:00 p.m. looking for shelter openings. All the shelters were full. With tears in his eyes, he told me to drop him off at his brother's job and he would sleep outside of the restaurant that night. When I dropped him off, I told him I would pick him up tomorrow and would make sure he got into a shelter for at least 30 days.

As I drove home, I thought to myself something had to be done for youth aging out of the foster care system. That evening, I tossed and turned all night laying in my bed thinking about the young man's safety. The next day I picked him up and we both went straight to Legislative Hall. A senator was able to get Antonio Rasin into a 30-day shelter that day. As a Mentor, it gave me 30 days to help the young man find employment and an apartment.

I taught him how to complete job applications, how to find work, how to make a living and understand household basics. He did get an apartment and a job. He was able to make a living and take care of himself. He shared his experience about me when speaking with Kimberly B. Gladney; "She basically taught me everything I know."

As I continued working with youth aging out of foster care, the Lord laid in my heart to open a transitional home for these youth in Delaware. I laughed – God, really? I am not business-minded; I am very shy, I do not like speaking in front of people. God, you know I failed speech class twice in college - I have no money, help or resources. The list went on and on.

Several months passed and the Lord spoke to me again to yield to the vision He gave me, to open a transitional home for young women who were aging out of the foster care system in Delaware. That night as I sat on the bed, I surrendered and yielded to God's plan.

I was very excited about the vision. My faith and confidence in God increased. I began saying I can do all things through Christ that strengthens me. I was very excited about the vision and told a friend what the Lord instructed me to do, but her response was negative. Her response was, "Can you really open a transitional home without money or resources?" She said that I never did it before, it would not work and it was impossible. When I got off the phone, I was tired of all the negativity. Feeling discouraged, I prayed to God to send positive friends in my life. Friends who would push me into my destiny!

I encourage you today to be very careful with whom you share your dreams! Remember what happened to Joseph in the Bible; he shared his dream with his brothers and they got angry and sold him. Not every person can comprehend who you are in God and what plans God has for your life. Surround yourself with positive people. People with FAITH! People with VISIONS and DREAMS! People who will inspire – empower, motivate and push you into your destiny!

You have to guard your mind against dream-killers and distance yourself from the small-minded and negative people who want to pull you down. Having positive relationships and the right people around you, will empower you to reach your highest potential in God.

Chapter Three
The Process

Growing up as a little girl, my heart's desire was to be married and have a family. I remember window shopping and looking at the beautiful wedding dresses and shoes! I was DREAMING the DREAM! Several years ago, I used to cut out pictures of wedding locations, food choices, decoration samples and wrote down colors for the bridesmaids - and the list went on and on. I was really creating a vision board for my DREAM wedding day!

One fine day, a friend introduced me to a handsome young man. At first, I was very excited and in my mind, I was thinking, "Finally my husband is here!" I did not wait for the friendship to build. During our phone conversations, everything was great; I thought about this person every day and night! I could not wait to speak to him. He started taking me out on dates and boy was he saying the right things! When he picked me up - he got out of his car, came around quickly and opened the door for me. When we arrived at the restaurant, he again got out of his car to open my door. He was such a *gentleman*. I loved that! He always made sure to open the door to let me in and out of a building and in or out of the car. I felt like a QUEEN! God, is he the o*ne* you have sent to me?

My interest in this young man grew very quickly. I decided to pray and ask God what role he played in my life. As I began to seek the face of God concerning this relationship, the young man began to distance himself. He distanced himself until many weeks went by without him calling me. I was so devastated. I cried my eyes out for a week. I was confused because it was as if this person fell off the earth and disappeared. We never had an argument or disagreement.

I was very confused. I remember praying in the prayer room, really asking God what went wrong - because as soon as I started praying, that is when this individual began to distance himself. I remember God speaking to me in the prayer room; "He is not the one that I sent." God stated that in this time of my singleness, "I need to live out the DREAMS He placed within me and live a life of purpose." After God spoke to me, I felt peace like never before.

A short time later, the Lord placed desire on my heart to read Exodus 4. Moses spent forty years on the backside of the desert, herding sheep and God called him to lead His people out of Egypt. Moses told God that the people might not believe nor listen to him. Moses did not have faith in himself. Moses believed he did not have any skills or abilities to lead God's people out of Egypt.

Moses felt that he was not worthy of God's call. God and Moses converse in Exodus 4:2, *"And the LORD said unto him, what is that in thine hand? And he said, a rod."* After mediating on Exodus 4, God spoke to me and said there is GREATNESS inside of me. God revealed that He had a purpose and a plan for my life and I needed to use what was in my hand. I was to use the gifts and talents He gave me in order to birth the DREAMS inside of me.

As I continued my spiritual walk with God, I found my identity. I began to feel comfortable with myself. I began to love myself, instead of looking for men to love me! I began to see what God sees! I learned not to wait for people to accept me, but know that God accepts me!

In 2008, K.I.S.H. (Kingdom Investments in Single Hearts) Home, Inc. was birthed. K.I.S.H. Home, Inc. is a nonprofit organization that empowers, inspires, heals and guides young girls and women in the community - as well as women who have aged-out of the foster-care system. One of the visions God gave me was the Women Destined for Greatness Mentoring Program, to serve as a catalyst of inspiration for young women to discover their self-worth, build their self-esteem and self-confidence.

God continued to order my steps and assigned the right people to mentor and volunteer for the mentoring programs. When the first workshop for the mentoring program occurred, only two girls attended. I was not happy about this number, but I kept going and hosting more workshops. As I continued, God gave me strategic ideas regarding how to market the workshops and events the organization hosted; it was then when the attendance numbers increased. Months passed, more girls and young women began attending the workshops and a couple of the organization events even sold out.

As you pursue your God-given dreams, you have to hold your head up and know that you are loved and appreciated by God. We have a unique and personal call upon our lives. Live for God and not for people! Be yourself; do not try to copy others. God created you for such a time as this. Colossians 1:16 says, *"For by Him all things were created, all things were created by Him and for Him."*

I would like to encourage you today that when you have a dream to pursue - pursue it, because with God all things are possible. If God gave you a vision, do not despise small beginnings. God will put His 'super' on top of your 'natural'. Dreamers, it is your time and season to COME FORTH! Come forth with your DREAMS in this year!

Take the limits off God! Do not be stopped by circumstances or ruled by FEAR! COME FORTH! God is calling you higher! It is time to BIRTH YOUR God-given DREAMS!

Chapter Four
Faith at Work

As I continued working on the transitional home vision, I was asking God how I would get the funds to open the transitional home. At the time, I was going to different grant workshops and during one of the presentations, they stated prayer would not be allowed if the organization was awarded money. From that point, I really began asking God for ways to bring in funding without taking Him out of the vision.

Then one day during prayer, the Lord placed in my heart to host a project to generate funds to assist with the transitional home. The non-profit had to come up with $1,000.00 in 30 days. At that time, I presented the vision to the board members. Half of the board members said it was possible to come up with the money, but the other half said it was not possible because the organization's bank account contained less than $100 dollars because we just started. One thing I know about God is that He is ALWAYS faithful and ALWAYS on time! Dreamers, you have to remember that when God gives instructions - follow them and be obedient because God does not move in the norm. God is a supernatural God.

During this time of believing God for the funds, I went before the Lord in prayer and meditated on the Word of God! All things are possible with God! The earth is the Lord's and the fullness there of. Ephesians 3:20 states, *"God can do exceedingly abundantly above all we can ask or think."* As week one approached - no money; as week two approached - no money. At this time, half of the board members on my side said it was impossible to get the $1,000.00. They stated it would never happen because it was too late. I did not let their statements stop me because I knew I heard from God. As week three approached, there was still no money. I continued praying and meditating on the Word of God. Week 4 was approaching, and we needed the money by the following Saturday.

God is full of surprises. He never answers our prayer the way we expect. We were pleasantly surprised! God is always on time in what He does. He has never been late. During week four, I received a phone call from a first lady at a local church who saw an article in the newspaper about the organization. She asked if I could speak about the organization at the Women's Conference. When I got off the phone, I wondered why anyone would want to hear anything about an organization at a Women's Conference.

The conference was held on a Saturday. When I finished speaking about the organization at this conference, a woman from the audience raised her hand and said she wanted to say something. She walked up to the front of the platform where I stood and stated that the Lord laid in her heart to donate $1,000.00 to the organization. When the young woman handed me the money, it was not a check, or money order - it was *cash*! Cash was just the form we needed because a check would have required time to clear and that we did not have. We needed the money to be available now. I began to cry with joy in front of the women in the audience and shared my testimony.

God proved Himself that day that He is *faithful* to His Word! I continued my journey to walk in His Best! I want to remind you that God loves you and has a purpose for your *life*! Through that experience, God was teaching me to trust and believe! That if He asks me to do anything pertaining to the vision and it seems impossible - I have to remember all things are possible with God!

God wants to bring us to a place of faith. Faith is active. It is not only good to believe - but you have to exert action. In the Bible, God showed Abram a vision that he would have children as many as the stars in the sky. At that time, Abram was in old age without children. Abram believed God! He had faith in God's promise. To have faith in God is to trust Him. Hebrews 11:1 says, *"Now faith is the substance of things hoped for the evidence of things not seen."* It is impossible to please God without faith. God moves by our faith.

God showed Himself faithful at the earlier stages of networking for the organization. I remember attending my first networking workshop for the organization. There were so many people there exchanging business cards, socializing and greeting one another. I felt like an outcast because this environment was so new to me.

As I looked around to find the nearest seat available, a woman approached me and introduced herself. She told me her name and shared information about her business. I smiled and nodded my head the whole time, but deep down inside I was praying, "God please put the words in my mouth so I can tell her about the organization with boldness and confidence." When she finished sharing details about her business, she asked me about my business. I took out my business card, a pamphlet and then started to share the mission and vision of the organization.

While I was explaining the organization to her, she had tears streaming down her face. The woman interrupted me and said with tears in her eyes that before she attended this workshop, she prayed to God for a divine connection. She said that she loved the mission and the vision. She also told me that she has money, but wanted to donate money to the right organization. We exchanged numbers and she kept her word. Months after, she donated a large amount of money towards the organization. God again showed up like never before.

DREAM BIGGER! Believe God! God wants to do great and mighty things in your life! God is restoring your hope! God is restoring your life! You are about to see the GLORY of God move in your life like NEVER before! Eyes have not seen nor have ears NOT heard! Everything the enemy has stolen from you, God is about to give it back to you and MORE!

Chapter Five
Dream Again

Several months after I disconnected myself from dream killers and began working on the vision, I remember sitting in my living room when the Lord gave me an assignment to host a fundraiser event for the non-profit organization. I was very excited about the project. I informed the board members and other people about the project. We started to plan four months ahead of the event.

Everything was going well, the vendors registered; we got the funds for the location and the fliers to advertise the event were ready for distribution. All tasks were completed for a successful event. The day of the event arrived, and I was very excited because in my mind, the team had done a GREAT job marketing the event and HUNDREDS of people would show up. The event started at 9:00 a.m. and by 2:00 p.m., only 30 people showed up to a facility that can hold over 500 people.

After the event, I went home extremely disappointed with tears in my eyes. I never wanted to get out of my bed again to face the board members or the world. In my eyes, the event was truly a flop and not successful. I felt like a BIG failure! I told myself I would never host another event again for the rest of my life.

One day during prayer, I cried out to God asking why the event was not successful and what I did wrong. The Lord laid in my heart that the event was a success because I completed the project. He reminded me that numbers did not matter; it was how the event laid out in excellence. The Lord also reminded me to DREAM again! Just because it did not work out the way I planned, does not mean it was not successful. God was teaching me to become successful; you have to learn from your failures - what and what not to do. Moreover, the more you do something - the better you will become. God was teaching me that He is guiding me, leading me and encouraging me not to give up and to Dream Big!

The following year, the Lord laid in my heart to host another fundraiser event. I began this time first by seeking the face of God for instructions and directions. I made many changes from things I did at the last event. I worked harder and marketed the event a different way than before. At this second event, we had over 200 people; there were more vendors and more tickets sold. The event was TRULY a BIG success! So, I want to encourage you today that when you have a dream - do not give up even if you lose money pursuing your dreams, people walking out on you, lack of support, etc. DREAM AGAIN and DREAM BIG!

For some of you reading this book, God showed you a vision of opening a business, publishing a book, writing songs, teaching, preaching, opening a shelter, writing plays, opening a non-profit, etc. and you ask God, "Can it really happen?" God is saying, *"Yes...if you only Believe!"* God wants to bring forth the DREAMER in YOU! Remember, with God all things are POSSIBLE! God wants us to DREAM outside of the box; Ephesians 3:20 states, *"Now unto us who is able to do exceeding abundantly above all that we ask or think; according to the power that worketh in us."* God's Word plainly and clearly states our purpose, which is to be God's hands on this earth. God wants you to succeed and if you are willing to step up to the plate, you will not fail - because God will never leave you nor forsake you.

To every dreamer reading this, I encourage you to DREAM AGAIN! When you have a dream - walk by faith and not by sight. The belief that dreams are impossible to achieve stops people from getting what they really want. People are what they believe themselves to be. Proverbs 23:7 says, *"For as he thinketh in his heart, so is he!"* If you want success, start thinking of yourself as a success. True success is the progressive achievement of your God-inspired goals. Success is the result of living in alignment with God's laws of success. God did not make you with limitations. Mark 9:23 says, *"All things are possible to him that believeth."* Believe that new and exciting opportunities are coming your way in this NEW SEASON because God is not through blessing you! Whatever vision God has showed you, believe His Word and step out in faith until it manifests in your life.

Chapter Six
Just Believe

There were seasons in my life when while pursuing my dreams, I asked God to guide me through my trials and tribulations. I remember one day, I was facing a situation that looked impossible! I had no money to buy food or items needed for my home. Even though I was working a full-time job, my money did not cover all of my expenses and food. I could not apply for food stamps because based on the system - I was making too much money. I was stuck. I cried out to the Lord to help me. In my mind, I was thinking I should call the guy I dated several years ago and he would send the money, but deep down inside, I could not do it. That week I remembered my daughter turning to me, saying, "Mommy, God will help us..."

During that week, I checked the mailbox; I normally do not check the mailbox every day because of all the bills, so I usually wait weeks before I check it. That week however, when I checked the mailbox - there was a check from a company stating they had over-charged me during the past few years and owed me money! When I opened the check, I cried and cried with joy knowing that God would supply my needs.

Dreamers, we have to know that everything depends on believing God. We cannot do anything without a living faith. If we only knew the power of God! The Word of God is life. God moves as you believe. Remember, "...*Faith is a substance; it is an evidence of things not seen*," (Hebrews 11:1). It brings about what you cannot see and brings forth what is not there. God took the Word and made the world in six days. God wants to bring us into that blessed place of faith - changing us into a real substance of faith, until we believe in our heart that whatever we ask, we believe we receive.

I love reading (Acts 6:8) because Stephen was truly a man of faith. God manifested Himself in Stephen's body so that he was full of faith and power and performed great wonders and signs among the people. God could do mighty things through him because he dared to believe God. God could fulfill His purpose through Stephen's life because he believed all things are possible with God.

As DREAMERS, God wants to do great things through your life in this season for His kingdom. There are assignments God has specifically called you to do that no one else in the world can do. God wants you to believe that all things are possible with Him. It does not matter where you are in life and if you feel stuck - believe that God can make every crooked way straight and that your steps are ordered. God's hands are upon you to birth your dreams.

You might feel like Daniel in the lion's den, or Shadrach, Meshach and Abednego thrown into the fire. Remember through the fire and the storm you will birth greatness. You will begin to see God move in your life like never before. The things you endured were to increase your faith in God. There are days when we as dreamers need to have our faith strengthened and we need to know God has designed the just to live by faith. We have to remember that God's Word is sufficient. One word from God can change a nation. God's Word is "from everlasting to everlasting." I believe God wants to bring you to a definite place of unwavering faith and confidence in Him as you pursue your God-given Dreams.

I remember working on a project and the non-profit had to come up with $2,000.00. I began to pray and continued to stand on the Word of God. Weeks went by and there was no sign that the organization would be able to come up with the money. One day while driving home, the Holy Spirit spoke to me and said to check the non-profit organization's mailbox. Now mind you, it was after 10:00 p.m. - but I listened and checked the mailbox. I want to encourage you dreamers - that when the Holy Spirit speaks to your heart, just obey.

Many times, we miss the blessing of God because we do not move when God speaks to us and our dreams are delayed. We have to move when God speaks the first time and things will flow better and easier in our lives. When I opened the mailbox, there was a letter from a company; inside the envelope, was a paper stating, "Here are ways you can receive funds by using our fundraising package." I put the package down, but the Holy Spirit told me to continue looking inside the envelope. I looked inside; there was another white envelope and when I finally opened the last envelope, inside was a $2,000.00 check. I began to scream and cry and said, "God THANK YOU! You are truly faithful to Your Word!"

So, I encourage every dreamer today that no matter what your bank account looks like right now - remember God will always give you provision for your vision. BELIEVE, BELIEVE, BELIEVE! God wants to move supernaturally in your life right now and show you that He is truly DREAMING through your eyes! With God, all things are possible! DREAM BIG!

Chapter Seven
Hold Fast to the Vision

Remember, hold fast to the VISION! God will give you the provision for your vision. I remember several years ago; the non-profit organization needed $500.00 to launch a new project within three months. In the natural, it seemed utterly impossible. The non-profit organization had to raise the money within a month. Doubt began to creep in my mind because time was running out and the organization did not raise half of the money for its upcoming project. The Lord reminded me in Genesis 18:14, which says, *"Is anything too hard for the Lord?"*

One day I received a phone call from a young woman who lived in the Caribbean and she noticed on Social Media all the things the non-profit organization had done for young women in Delaware. She stated that she wanted to help and that the Lord laid on her heart to donate $500.00.

Be encouraged today that when you have a DREAM, remember that God is without limits! There is NOTHING too HARD FOR THE LORD! God starts with an impossible situation, because when the dream comes to pass, God will get all the credit and people will see the hands of God.

Remember when......

- God fed the Israelites... He sent manna
- David was able to kill Goliath the giant, with one sling shot and five smooth stones
- God closed the mouths of lions in the lion's den with Daniel
- God parted the Red Sea for the Israelites to cross
- God miraculously multiplied the supply of the widow
- God needed a Savior for the world, He created a baby in the virgin womb of Mary

No matter how impossible your circumstances may look, God is able to do exceedingly and abundantly above all that we ask or think! GOD IS ABLE! HOLD FAST TO THE VISION and believe in God's timing "...*though it tarry wait for it because it will surely come,*" (Habakkuk 2:3 KJV).

As I continued moving forward with my dreams, God instilled more ideas and strategies to help fund the vision. I began to create books, stage plays, music, a magazine company, Empowering workshops, a Dreamers' Movement Empowerment Tour, Empowerment Conference Call and empowering events.

I encourage every dreamer who began his or her VISON, but has yet to see the manifestation; look not to the right nor to the left, keep your eyes FIXED on God because He is a God that does not lie. Be encouraged and HOLD FAST TO THE VISION! If God showed you a vision, it will truly come to pass! Do not worry about how long it is taking to manifest. Remember God is always on time. God is making your crooked ways straight. You will be at the right place at the right time and God will divinely connect you with people who will help you with your vision.

KEEP DREAMING & KEEP PUSHING! Do not give up and do not give in! No matter what your circumstances may be, remember there is GREATNESS inside of you! God placed gifts and talents inside of you to make an impact in the world, for His Kingdom for such a time as this. This is the season to STEP out on FAITH! Pick your DREAM back up. There are no limitations with God! God has no limits! This is your season for new breakthrough new favor, new blessings, manifestation and dominion, new dreams, opened doors, divine connections and new opportunities for success! It is TIME to bring forth the DREAMER in YOU!

Chapter Eight
God Is All You Need

I remember several years ago, while pursuing my dreams, I was going through a 'Red-Sea experience'. I was recently laid off my job, my money was at its lowest point and I did not know how I was going to care for my child and myself. I thought my dreams were over because I had NEVER experienced anything like this in my life. I remember crying out to God because He told me to leave a guy who was paying all my bills and now, I was stuck in a dry place in my life. I had no family members in Delaware to assist me.

I called my mom to assist me with paying my rent. I had no money and did not want to become homeless. As I was speaking to my mom on the phone, she said, "I'm sorry I can't help you." On the other end of the phone I thought, I know my mom has money. Why is she acting like this? Little did I realize God was showing me that He is ALL I need and to use the rod - which is the Word of God. God showed me the

Scriptures, Exodus 14:13-16. As I read the text, the Israelites finally left Egypt but still there was a big problem. The Red Sea was in front of them and Pharaoh's army was approaching from behind. With the Red Sea in front of them and the Egyptians army behind them, it was literally being between a 'rock and a hard place.'

Moses had two choices - FAITH or FEAR. Moses chose faith and believed what God spoke to him. God told him to use what was in his hand, which was a rod and He Stretched out his rod towards the Red Sea and TRUSTED and OBEYED God. God performed the miracle, He parted the Red Sea and the Israelites were able to cross the sea.

After reading the verse, I began to pray that week, seeking the face of God in my prayer room with fasting and praying. One day while praying, the Lord instructed me to go to a place and they would give me the money to pay for rent. At first I thought, "How will they just give me money for my rent when they don't know me?" However, the Lord spoke to my heart and said, "Walk by faith and NOT by sight."

That day, I put on my clothes and went to the location where God instructed. When I arrived to the office, I explained to them that I was out of work and needed assistance with my rent. After hearing my story, the director of the organization informed me they do not usually assist people with their rent without an advance appointment and without being a member of their organization. However, the director stated there was something different about me so he wanted to help.

I left the location that day with the money I needed for my rent. When I arrived home, I had tears in my eyes and my heart was filled with joy! God spoke to me and said, "*God is all you NEED.*" Some of you DREAMERS are going through a Red-Sea experience right now in your life. You might feel like your back is against the wall and there is no hope left. You feel like when you take one-step forward - something comes up and knocks you twenty steps backwards. It seems like you make efforts but never see the fruition because there is always an obstacle in your way.

I want to encourage you today - God is saying do not look at your circumstances, keep your eyes focused on Jesus. What man says is impossible - God says all things are POSSIBLE! Do not look to the right or to the left! Hold on, help is on its way! Do not be AFRAID! Trust God! He will see you through! God is fighting for you even when you feel as if no one is there. Stop stressing over your bills or if you don't have enough money in the bank; if the doctors diagnose you with a sickness or if you lost your job, home, car or if your DREAMS seem dead. Keep standing and believing the Word of God and YOUR situation will change! Have FAITH in GOD! Remember, God got this! Cast all your cares on the Lord, for He cares for YOU!

As I continued to pursue my dreams, I noticed my face and throat were swollen. Initially, I figured I was gaining weight and needed to watch what I was eating. One day, I went for an annual checkup and the doctor looked at me and stated my neck looked enlarged. He said I had to take some tests to make sure everything was okay. When I took the tests, the results came back that I had large tumors in my throat, which had to be removed immediately. If not, they would cause great damage because the tumors were multiplying and increasing.

While at the doctor's one day, he informed me that he needed to remove the tumors - but wanted to advise me that if he made a mistake during the surgery and cut the wrong vein while removing the tumors, I would not be able to speak again. I told the doctor I needed time to think about it because I use my voice a lot and could not afford to stop talking. That night, I laid in the bed crying out to God because it just did not make sense. The devil began to torment me and said, "NOW I will silence you forever. You will not be able to speak again; you will have to use sign language to speak to people. Your dreams, life and destiny are OVER!"

During that season of my life, I could not tell anyone what I was going through. I had to stay very close to God to hear His directions and plans for me. One day during prayer, the Lord laid on my heart to go forth with the procedure to remove the tumors. I felt peace.

The devil continued to torment my mind and saying that I would NEVER finish the dreams God had placed within me. Two months later, I contacted the doctor and set up an appointment for my surgery. The night before the surgery, the Lord spoke to me and said all is well and that the surgery will be a success and I will be able to speak. God spoke to me and said that I will birth EVERY dream He placed in my heart and not to fear or worry. The day of the surgery, there were many nurses who greeted me - but one particular nurse came to my bedside before the surgery; he said he would assist the doctor to make sure he did not cut the wrong vein. Tears began to flow down my face and I felt the peace of God.

After the surgery, I opened eyes and my mother was by my bedside. The doctor came by my bedside to check on me and test my voice. He called my name and I answered. I began to cry with tears of joy because the Lord kept His Word and His PROMISES over my life. Some of you DREAMERS today are going through a difficult circumstance which seems out of your control and overwhelming. You must realize there are some battles that you simply cannot fight - and should not fight in your own strength. Sometimes God tells us to take our positions, stand still and see His deliverance. Sometimes we need to take our hands off, stand back and let God fight for us.

We should not fear what comes against us but stand firm in our FAITH. God knows the whole situation. God knows what we will go through before we go through it! We need to let God have control and fight the battle we are facing. He has promised that He is with us and that He will bring us through! I would like to encourage you today that God wants you to walk in His BEST! No matter what your life circumstances looks like right now! God wants you to birth the dreams He gave you to make a difference in the world for such a time as this!

When God shows you the vision, He wants you to walk by faith and trust Him! Do not look to the right or to the left; keep your eyes on Jesus! God will guide you! He will give you all the directions you need to accomplish your dreams! God wants to do great things in your life! Remember that you are truly destined for greatness and there is greatness inside of you!

Chapter Nine
A Vision Becomes Reality

Every God-given vision will become real if we have patience. Visions are about God's will and not about us. Godly visions can be frightening because they are so great. However, they become reality as we move in faithfulness. God gives great visions that only God can accomplish so that when they become reality - God must receive all the glory!

In the Bible, Paul had a vision known as the Macedonian call. God gave Paul a large vision! The first thing Paul did when he got the vision, "he endeavoured to fulfil it immediately". Paul was assured that the vision and the call were of God. With a vision, you need to be able to see the dreams God is bringing about in our lives and say, "Yes, God is in it." You have to remember if God is the source of your vision, then you will need God to fulfill it. One key point is that God's vision ALWAYS benefits all humanity.

The year was 2009 when I really began working on getting the transitional home up and running. I met someone who was very knowledgeable about youth aging out of the foster-care system in Delaware. I was advised to contact an agency that would assist me with creating a business plan. I remember attending the first meeting and my mentor was very knowledgeable about opening profit businesses and non-profits.

My mentor gave me an assignment to write down my mission, vision, goals and the programs the non-profit would offer, etc. I was very excited about this new journey. I remember going home and writing my business plan in one day and it was only one page.

The next week I met with my mentor; he took one look at the business plan and ripped it to pieces in my face. He said it was not acceptable and that I needed to remain focused on the vision. One thing my mentor stated which was very profound was that a business plan is like a Bible. The Bible is a guide for us as we live on earth; the business plan is also a guide that when I die - the vision will live on and not die with me. My mentor also stated that if I do not write the business plan correctly, no one will be able to run with the vision and I would not leave a legacy.

I went home that day and cried and cried. I told God this was too hard for me and I wasn't sure if I had enough knowledge to put the business plan together. God began speaking to me in my prayer time and said that I needed to seek Him for the mission, vision and layout of the transitional home. The same week, I stayed in my prayer room longer and waiting for instructions from God. Weeks passed, and the Lord began clearly revealing the mission, vision, purpose, programs and goals for the transitional home. The following month when I met with my mentor, he was very impressed with the layout of the business plan. My business plan was 38 pages and very detailed. I had pictures of a vision of the transitional home.

As I sought the Lord in prayer, I realized I needed a name for the non-profit. One day at work at my corporate job, I was speaking to my co-worker, Mrs. Annette Cooper; I told her I had half of the name for the non-profit but needed a beginning for the name. Then out of her mouth, she said, "The name of the nonprofit is KISH." I said, "Oh no, I don't want anything close to my name at all." She then looked me straight in my eyes and said, "It's KISH." I knew she was truly a woman of God and she knew the voice of God.

On that same day when I got home, I asked the Lord for confirmation about the name. That week, the Lord spoke and said it is K.I.S.H., which stands for (Kingdom Investments in Single Hearts).

- **Kingdom**: The Kingdom of God will be built through the ministry of K.I.S.H. Home, Inc. by incorporating programs that will encourage girls and young women to make an impact in the world.

- **Investments**: An investment of time and life enrichment activities that will be implemented in such a way to empower girls and young women to change their lives.

- **Single**: Empowering single girls and single women.

- **Hearts**: Helping girls and young women discover their potential in becoming world-changing leaders by pursuing their God-given dreams, goals and visions.

That day I thanked God for the revelation. After God revealed the name, I asked Him to show me the people He would like to have as Board Members and Board of Advisors. God began showing me different people's faces in the prayer room and when I said I wanted them to sit on the Board, they said yes.

As time went on, different newspapers recognized the nonprofit organization throughout Delaware, for creating a transitional home for young women who have aged out of the foster care system. I began sharing my story via radio shows, magazines and television concerning the vision God gave me to assist these young women. In my mind, I thought the money would pour in now that I was sharing the vision via various media outlets. However, God reminded me that His thoughts are not my thoughts and His ways are not my ways. The way HE chooses to release the funds for the home will come His way.

In my prayer time, the Lord laid in my heart to work on a book project that would bring in funds for the start of the transitional home. I was very excited about the book project, but while working on the book project - I became ill to the point where it was hard for me to walk. I went to the doctor and he said I had tumors in my uterus that needed to be removed.

I went home crying because I did not know how I was going to finish everything I needed to accomplish for the book signing. The Lord spoke to me and said to trust Him and lean not to my own understanding and that everything would work out. The book signing was two months away from my surgery. The day of my surgery, I was very nervous because anything could have gone wrong. I remember saying a prayer as the nurses wheeled me into the operating room. My fear was that I would not wake up after the surgery and would never fulfill my dreams. The Lord spoke to me and said He had too much work for me to do for Him and that I would not die on the operating table. I would be fine.

During the surgery, the doctor removed ten large tumors from my uterus and the surgery was successful. When I opened my eyes, it was as if God was saying to me, "I told you that you are going to be alright." During my weeks of recovery, I continued to work - even on days I was in pain. I continued to push and stayed focused working on the layout of the book-signing event and it was a success.

I continued working on other projects to generate funds to open the transitional homes. Years went by and I began to get tired because I was not seeing anything coming together and the home was not up and running. Then one day the Lord laid in my heart to start creating a detailed layout of the items I would need in the transitional home. I began to layout the items needed for the kitchen, living room, bathrooms, staff office and resident's rooms. I also worked on the colors for the bathrooms, the kitchen, living room and bedrooms. Layout for the staff's office included the desk, paper, copier machine, computers, pens, and staples, etc.

As I wrote the details, I asked God why I was doing all of this because I didn't have the home yet nor had a location to move into - but the Lord told me to keep on writing the layout. I worked on the layout for the transitional home for two months. Four months after the transitional home layout was completed, the Lord laid in my heart to contact a company that owned different properties within the State of Delaware. When I spoke to the office manager, I informed her about the vision I had in opening a transitional home for youth aging out of foster care. She was very excited about the vision and stated that she had a property with three-bedrooms, kitchen, two full bathrooms and living room.

I set up an appointment that week to see the home and fell in love with it. It was just the right location. The size of the home was just what I needed to start my first transitional home. The following week, I called the office manager and informed her I was interested in the home. She gave me the housing application and told me how much was required for the down payment. The following week I had the KEYS to the HOME! K.I.S.H. Home, Inc. Transitional Living Home came to life on April 25, 2015. Glory to God! When I walked in the home, I laid on the floor and tears ran down my face with joy. The VISION became a REALITY! God is truly FAITHFUL to His Word! Include God in everything. All things are possible with Him.

I could not have gotten rid of my insecurities, low-self-esteem and lack of self-confidence to bloom to have self-confidence and being such a *dreamer* that I am today! I have evolved from being such a doubter to who I am today. That is to be confident and to pursue my purpose here on earth. I became a dreamer, all that I can be by the grace of God for Him. I found my purpose and who I am to make a difference for the Kingdom of God.

I want to encourage every DREAMER today that your DREAMS will come to PASS! Remember, giving up is NOT an option! It is YOUR time to DREAM BIG! It is your time to take LEAPS of FAITH and pursue your God-given DREAMS! Do not get discouraged! Do not look at your age! Do not look at how long the dreams are taking to manifest! Keep the faith and BELIEVE God! In this NEW SEASON, you are coming from been a DOUBTER to becoming a DREAMER! No more fear! No more delay! You will pursue your DREAMS in this SEASON with boldness and confidence knowing that all things are POSSIBLE with God! It is your time to BRING FORTH THE DREAMER in YOU! DREAM BIG!

Prophetic Release and Mediation Scriptures

Prophetic Release for Dreamers

- God is saying in this SEASON...

- Your GIFT will continue to make ROOM for YOU in this SEASON!

- HOLD ON! You are one day CLOSER to seeing your God-given DREAMS COME to PASS!

- Your NAME is being carried in the WIND! God is ABOUT to MOVE in your life like NEVER BEFORE!

- DREAM BIGGER in this SEASON! You are about to birth SOMETHING so GREAT that will make such an IMPACT!

- After you PRAY in FAITH...EXPECT the MANIFESTATION!

- In this NEW SEASON...God is ABOUT to take you places where you have never been!

- In this NEW SEASON...You are ABOUT to walk into OVERFLOW!

- It's COMING SUDDENLY for YOU in this NEW SEASON!

- God has DIVINE connections COMING to you in this SEASON that will change your LIFE!

- God is ABOUT to TURN your DREAMS into REALITY in this NEW SEASON!

- Prepare for the thing YOU have asked for! It's ABOUT to COME to PASS in this SEASON!
- Hold ON! Investors are LOOKING to CONNECT with you this SEASON! God is BRINGING THEM into YOUR PATH!
- Hold On! You shall experience BREAKTHROUGH after BREAKTHROUGH after BREAKTHROUGH in this NEW SEASON!
- Your latter shall be GREATER than the former!
- God is going to ACCELERATE YOU in this NEW SEASON!
- God is ABOUT to give you great FAVOR in this SEASON as you birth your DREAMS!
- Angels have been deployed to assist you with your DREAMS!
- GET READY! DOOR after DOOR after DOOR will be opened for YOU in this NEW SEASON like NEVER BEFORE!
- In this SEASON, God is going to move in YOUR life in such a way, YOU will think it's a DREAM! God will blow your mind!
- God is ABOUT to give you SEVEN STREAMS of INCOME to FUND YOUR VISION!
- You truly need to PREPARE for the #WEALTH that is about to #MANIFEST in your life!
- YOUR territory is ABOUT to be expanded GLOBALLY in this NEW SEASON!
- God shall surely do it for YOU in this NEW SEASON!
- Expect EXPANSION in this NEW SEASON!

- NO more DELAYS! God is ABOUT to LAUNCH you OUT in this SEASON!

- Tomorrow about this time, THINGS ARE GOING TO CHANGE for YOU!

- You will know it was no one but GOD who did it for you in this NEW SEASON!

- DREAM BIGGER in this SEASON! God has BIG plans for your life! TRUST and BELIEVE!

20 Bible Verses to Meditate on When Working on Your Dreams!

1. But they that wait upon the LORD shall renew their strength; they shall mount up with wings as eagles; they shall run, and not be weary; and they shall walk, and not faint. **Isaiah 40:31**

2. Blessed is the man that trusteth in the LORD, and whose hope the LORD is. **Jeremiah 17:7**

3. And Jesus said unto them, Because of your unbelief: for verily I say unto you, If ye have faith as a grain of mustard seed, ye shall say unto this mountain, Remove hence to yonder place; and it shall remove; and nothing shall be impossible unto you. **Matthew 17:20**

4. Now unto him that is able to do exceeding abundantly above all that we ask or think, according to the power that worketh in us, **Ephesians 3:20**

5. But his delight is in the law of the LORD; and in his law doth he meditate day and night. And he shall be like a tree planted by the rivers of water, that bringeth forth his fruit in his season; his leaf also shall not wither; and whatsoever he doeth shall prosper. **Psalm 1:2-3**

6. There are many devices in a man's heart; nevertheless the counsel of the LORD, that shall stand. **Proverbs 19:21**

7. The counsel of the LORD standeth for ever, the thoughts of his heart to all generations. **Psalm 33:11**

8. And Jabez called on the God of Israel, saying, Oh that thou wouldest bless me indeed, and enlarge my coast, and that thine hand might be with me, and that thou wouldest keep me from evil, that it may not grieve me! And God granted him that which he requested. **1 Chronicles 4:10**

9. Grant thee according to thine own heart, and fulfil all thy counsel. **Psalm 20:4**

10. Get wisdom, get understanding: forget it not; neither decline from the words of my mouth. **Proverbs 4:5**

11. Delight thyself also in the LORD: and he shall give thee the desires of thine heart. **Psalm 37:4**

12. Trust in the LORD with all thine heart; and lean not unto thine own understanding. In all thy ways acknowledge him, and he shall direct thy paths. **Proverbs 3:5-6**

13. Without counsel purposes are disappointed: but in the multitude of counsellors they are established. **Proverbs 15:22**

14. A man's heart deviseth his way: but the LORD directeth his steps. **Proverbs 16:9**

15. And the LORD answered me, and said, Write the vision, and make it plain upon tables, that he may run that readeth it.For the vision is yet for an appointed time, but at the end it shall speak, and not lie: though it tarry, wait for it; because it will surely come, it will not tarry. **Habakkuk 2:2-3**

16. But seek ye first the kingdom of God, and his righteousness; and all these things shall be added unto you. **Matthew 6:33**

17. And all things, whatsoever ye shall ask in prayer, believing, ye shall receive. **Matthew 21:22**

18. But Jesus beheld them, and said unto them, With men this is impossible; but with God all things are possible. **Matthew 19:26**

19. I can do all things through Christ which strengtheneth me. **Philippians 4:13**

20. The thoughts of the diligent tend only to plenteousness; but of every one that is hasty only to want. **Proverbs 21:5**

Dreamers Prophetic Prayer
I Declare and Decree......

* You will take GREAT leaps of faith as you pursue your God-given dreams.

* In this season you will USE what is in YOUR HAND!

* God will download strategies and ideas for your dreams.

* GOD WILL SUPERNATURALLY OPEN DOORS! You will be at the right place at the right time!

* GOD WILL BLESS YOU WITH DIVINE CONNECTIONS and SUPERNATURAL RESOURCES!

* You will have UNCOMMON FAVOR over your life!

* You will have NEW OPPORTUNITIES!

* It will be a YEAR of INCREASE!

* It will be a YEAR of the OVERFLOW!

* There will be NO more LACK!

* By this time NEXT YEAR, your life will NEVER be the same!

Living Your Dreams Journal

Write down all the dreams you would like to achieve this year.

What is the mission for your dream?

What is the vision for your dream?

What are your passions?

What steps are you willing take to pursue your dreams?

What obstacles have you already overcame as you pursue your dreams?

Create a vision board of pictures of your dreams this year.

Write down what pictures you will use for your vision board as a guide

_____
_____
_____
_____
_____
_____
_____
_____
_____
_____
_____
_____
_____
_____
_____
_____
_____
_____
_____

Write down Scriptures for you to meditated on, while pursing your Dreams

Write out some goals you would like to accomplish within 1 month, 3 months, 6 months and 12 months

One Month

Three Months

Six Months

Twelve Months

Words have Power. For the next 7 days before you go to bed, Write down the words you spoke over your life during the day.

Day 1

_____
_____
_____
_____
_____
_____

Day 2

_____
_____
_____
_____

Day 3

Day 4

Day 5

Day 6

Day 7

_____
_____
_____
_____
_____
_____
_____

Look through what you wrote for the last 7 days. Have you been speaking more positive or negative over your life?

About Dr. Kishma A. George

Dr. Kishma A. George can, in a single phrase, be described as a Purpose Pusher. She is an evangelist, entrepreneur, inspirational speaker, radio personality, mentor, playwright, producer and author, and her overarching mission is to inspire people to fulfill their God-given purpose. She believes that despite life's circumstances, there is greatness inside of you! Dr. Kishma's work as a speaker and mentor is executed through the Women Destined for Greatness Mentoring Program in Kent County, Delaware.

Dr. Kishma A. George is the President and CEO of K.I.S.H. (Kingdom Investments in Single Hearts) Home, Inc. K.I.S.H. Home, Inc. was founded out of the desire to make an impact in the lives of girls and women in Delaware, as well as those young women who are presently in, or have aged out of the foster care system. Dr. George worked as an Independent Living Mentor witnessed the tremendous challenges of aged out foster care youth experienced while trying to find their way to a self- sufficient and stable life.

A passion within her grew for these young adults and their future as she experienced their frustration in handling basic skills, such as opening a checking/savings account, parenting and the frustration of single parenthood. Dr. Kishma wants to make a difference in their lives and make certain that they have a safe, successful transition to adulthood and independent living.

Her diligence and passion for young women have been recognized in various newspaper articles, including the Dover Post, Delaware News Journal, Delaware State News, and Milford Beacon. She was also featured in the Kingdom Voices Magazine, Gospel 4 U Magazine, K.I.S.H. Magazine, BOND Inc., and BlogSpot's week spotlight "Fostered Out of Love". In addition to appearing as special, guest on the Atlanta LIVE TV Show, Life Talk Radio Show with Coach TMB, Live TV Show Straight Talk for Women Only, and The Frank and Travis Radio Show on Praise 105.1.

Empowered Women Ministries have recognized Dr. Kishma as Woman of the Year in the category of Entrepreneurial Success, as well as Zeta Phi Beta Sorority, Inc. / Theta Zeta Zeta Chapter for her outstanding involvement in the Greater Dover Community. She was also presented with the Diversity Award (2013) from the State of Delaware / Social Services, the Authentic Servant Leadership Award (2014) & New Castle County Chapter of the DSU Alumni Association 33rd annual Scholarship Luncheon for outstanding service to the Wilmington Community and the Delaware State University (2014), Church Girlz Rock(2015); Humanitarian Award (2015), Faith Fighter Award (2016) , Business Woman of the Year (2016), CHOICES "Woman of the Year" (2016) and Global Smashers Award (2017).

Dr. Kishma received her Bachelor of Science degree in Psychology from Delaware State University & an Honorary Doctorate of Philosophy; Humane Letters from CICA International University & Seminary. Her passion is to empower you through the Word of God and inspire you to begin living your DREAMS. No matter what your circumstances may be, God has a purpose for your life.

Dr. Kishma strives to make a difference in your life and make certain that YOU will birth EVERY DREAM God has placed on the inside. *Dr. Kishma A. George is the Director of Women Destined for Greatness Mentoring Program and Visionary/Editor-in-Chief for K.I.S.H. Magazine.*

To Contact Kishma A. George visit www.kishmageorge.com.

Acknowledgements

First and foremost, I want to give God all the glory and honor, as He made this vision possible. I love You Lord with all my heart! 🖤

In memory of my beloved father, Edmond Felix George; I am thankful for his encouragement and inspiring me to dream. 🖤

To the best mother in the world, Novita Scatliffe-George; I thank you for your love, support, encouraging words and praying for me. Thank you for not giving up on me. I love you Mom! 🖤

To my wonderful daughter Kiniquá, I love you dearly. Thank you for your encouraging words, hugs and love. 🖤

To my family; James, Raeisha, Christopher, Joshua, Seriah, Janisha and Kayla - thank you for supporting the vision with your prayers and love. 🖤

Thank you, Toy James, Ronisha Williams and Abena Mc Clean for your prayers, support and encouraging me to pursue my dreams. I thank God that you are my special friends. Love you ladies 🖤

A special thank you to Apostle Regina Martin for letting God use you to remind me it's time to birth the book inside of me. Thank you for been an inspiration to me and so many people. Love and blessings 🖤

A special thank you to Prophetess Ronisha Williams, Elder Leandra Green for your prayers, encouraging words and supporting the vision. Thank you for believing in me. Love you ladies 🖤

A Special thank you my beautiful Jackie Hicks for her amazing photography, beautiful Letitia Thornhill for her gift of makeup artistry, beautiful Sonja Alston for an amazing hairstyle!! Love you ladies! 🖤

To K.I.S.H. Home, Inc.'s Board/Advisors, Volunteers and Mentors; thank you for your dedication, support and believing in the vision of helping make a difference in the lives of young women in Delaware.

To Les Brown, thank you for all your support and encouraging words.

To Serena Brown-Travis, thank you for all your support and encouraging words.

To Emily Ann Warren, thank you for your support, love, and believing in me.

To Pastor Ayanna, Publisher; I thank God, every day for bringing you into my life. You have been a blessing. Thank you for your encouraging words, support, love and believing in the vision. Love you ♥

Lastly, but not least I would like to thank CTS graphics, Chosen Butterfly Publishing and everyone who encouraged, prayed for and supported K.I.S.H. Home, Inc. over the years, I am forever grateful. God Bless!

About K.I.S.H. Home, Inc.

Kingdom Investments in Single Hearts (K.I.S.H.) Home, Inc. was founded in August 2008 out of the desire to make an impact in the lives of girls & women in the community as well as those young women who are presently in, or have aged out of the foster care system in Delaware. Through Ms. George works as an Independent Living Mentor, she has mentored young adults. During her tenure as a mentor, she witnessed the tremendous challenges these young people experienced while trying to find their way to a self-sufficient and stable life.

A passion within her grew for these young adults and their future as she experienced their frustration in handling basic skills, such as opening a checking/savings account, parenting and the frustration of single parenthood. Ms. George knew that these young adults, whether they were a single parent or single, needed a strong support system that would empower and encourage them to take control of their lives. They struggled in their transition of leaving their homes or foster care because many were still attending high school and were not emotionally or financially stable.

After witnessing this, Ms. George began her journey of seeking ways to assist young adults in becoming emotionally and economically self- sufficient so that their transition out of their homes or the foster care system and into independent living was successful. Many of the young adults with whom she worked with left their homes or foster care at 18 years old and found themselves homeless, pregnant, lacking self-esteem, incarcerated, unemployed and without guidance. As a mentor, Ms. George became frustrated by the minimum amount of resources the community offered these young adults. She wanted to make a difference in their lives and make certain that they had a safe, successful transition to adulthood and independent living.

K.I.S.H. Home, Inc. offers young women in Delaware the support they need to become emotionally stable and self-sufficient in every aspect of their lives and community.

Once again K.I.S.H. Home Inc. would like to thank you for the purchase of this book. Portions of the Proceeds will be going to K.I.S.H. Home Inc. a 501 (c) 3 non-profit, faith-based organization that is currently providing a 24-hour supervised residential home for young women ages 18-23 who are homeless, or have aged out of the foster care system in Delaware. If you would like to help make this transition home to expand you can send your donations to K.I.S.H. Home, Inc. P. O. BOX 672, Felton, DE 19943 or www.kishhomeinc.org.

www.ingramcontent.com/pod-product-compliance
Lightning Source LLC
Chambersburg PA
CBHW060042230426
43661CB00004B/627